Cambridge English Readers

Level 2

Series editor: Philip Prowse

Dead Cold

Sue Leather

CAMBRIDGE
UNIVERSITY PRESS

CAMBRIDGE UNIVERSITY PRESS
Cambridge, New York, Melbourne, Madrid, Cape Town, Singapore, São Paulo

Cambridge University Press
The Edinburgh Building, Cambridge CB2 2RU, UK

www.cambridge.org
Information on this title: www.cambridge.org/9780521693790

First published 2006

Sue Leather has asserted her right to be identified as the Author
of the Work in accordance with the Copyright, Design and Patents Act 1988.

Printed in India by Thomson Press (India) Limited

Illustrations by Paul McCaffery

A catalogue record for this publication is available from the British Library

ISBN-13 978-0-521-69379-0 paperback
ISBN-10 0-521-69379-9 paperback

ISBN-13 978-0-521-69392-9 paperback plus audio CD
ISBN-10 0-521-69392-6 paperback plus audio CD

Contents

People in the story

Flick Laine: a detective in the Denver Police
Leo Cohn: Chief of Denver Police – Flick's boss
Bill Gershon: Chief of Pine Crest Police
Teresa Douglas and Jeff Mason: students from Texas
Susan Hunter: a movie star

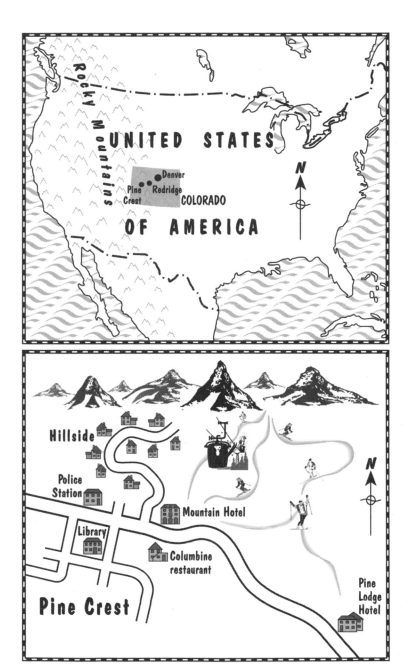

5

Chapter 1   *A body*

In January they found the girl's body.

They found it in Pine Crest. Pine Crest is a small town about 90 miles from Denver, in the Rocky Mountains. In the past it was famous for silver and gold. But now it's a place where people go on vacation; they ski there in the winter and walk in the mountains in the summer. Movie stars have homes there. It's beautiful and it's quiet when the snow falls. And the snow falls a lot in the winter. Pine Crest isn't usually the kind of place you find a dead body. Denver's the place for that, not Pine Crest.

Oh, of course sometimes there are skiing accidents, like in all ski resorts. I remember that a young man died about three years ago. He was skiing too fast and he went into a tree. It's sad, but it happens. But murder – killing someone – well, that's different.

So that January morning my boss, Leo Cohn, Chief of the Denver Police, called me into his office.

'Girl's body in Pine Crest, Flick,' said Leo. Leo was thin and worked too much. He never sat down. Now, he was standing near his desk. 'They found her yesterday.'

'Oh?' I said.

'It looks like someone killed her,' he said. I didn't say anything. 'Murder,' he said, as if I didn't understand. I waited. He didn't look at me. Then he said, 'I want you to go to Pine Crest.'

'Ha!' I said. 'So that's what you want. But Leo, why me? It's too soon. It was just two months ago … I can't!'

'Flick, you're the best,' he said, 'and you need to get out of Denver … it's the best thing.'

'Listen, Leo …' I started, but I stopped. Leo looked me in the eyes.

'Come on, Flick. Bill Gershon, the Chief of Police there, is an old friend of mine. He's not happy. If it's murder, it's bad for business. No-one wants to ski when there's a killer about.'

Well, yeah, I thought, as I looked out of Leo's window at the city, a dead body was bad for business. I knew Pine Crest. I used to go skiing there on the weekends. The town made its money from the thousands of visitors who went there every year. The restaurants, cafés, hotels, ski school, all made money from the people who went to beautiful Pine Crest for their vacation.

'And the girl?' I asked. 'Was she a visitor?'

Leo smiled. He could see that I was interested. 'Yes,' he said. 'She was there on a skiing vacation with some friends from college. Someone found her in the swimming pool at the hotel where she was staying.'

'She died in the swimming pool?' I asked. 'I mean ...'

'Looks like somebody drowned her,' Leo said.

I looked at him.

'She was twenty-three years old,' Leo said softly.

'And?' I asked.

'You'll get what you need from Gershon,' said Leo.

I got up to leave.

'Oh, and Flick ...' said Leo. I turned at the door.

'I want you to get this one and I want you to get it fast,' he said. 'First because it'll make the Denver Police Department look good. And we need that.'

'And second because you think it's good for me to get out of the office and back to work?' I said.

Leo didn't say anything, but it was true. He was helping me in his way.

'OK, Leo,' I said, 'but remember, it was just November, just two months ago ... that Scott ...'

'Yeah, yeah, I know. But Flick, Scott's dead,' said Leo. His voice was kind, but strong. 'And you've got to live.' He turned away from me and looked out of the window. Leo was finished.

I walked to my office to get the things I needed for a few days out of town: my notebook, cell phone and car keys. I thought about November, thought about Scott. Detective Scott King of the Denver Police. Then I took my gun and put it under my jacket.

I went downstairs to the parking lot. Scott and I worked together for four years. We were the best, the best the Denver Police Department had. We loved catching killers, robbers, all of Denver's criminals. But we were more than that, we were friends too. Scott was my best friend. Then one stupid, cold day in November, Eddie Lang killed Scott. And I saw my best friend die.

'Yeah,' I thought, 'Scott's dead and I've got to live.' Most days it was difficult.

I shook my head and Scott's face went away. I took my keys out of the pocket of my jacket and looked at the most beautiful car in the world, my red 1957 Chevrolet. My Chevy. I smiled. That car always made me smile. Some days it felt like it was the only good thing in my life.

I drove home fast to my apartment on Alameda, went in and packed a bag. I changed into my blue suit and looked at myself in the mirror in the bathroom. I looked OK. I looked like I came from the big city. I felt my gun inside my jacket. I was ready. Ready to find a killer ... without Scott.

Fifteen minutes later I was driving on I70 to Pine Crest, Colorado. I was trying to forget about Scott. And I was trying to forget about Eddie Lang.

Chapter 2 *Pine Crest*

Scott King. Yeah, it was hard to forget. As I drove up into the Rocky Mountains pictures came into my head. The first time we worked together, his smile, the things he said.

'Stop it, Flick!' I said to myself. I turned on the car radio. It was an old country song.

Then the news came on. 'Good morning, listeners,' said the voice. 'It's ten o'clock and here's the news. Police found a young woman's body in a swimming pool at the Mountain Hotel in Pine Crest yesterday. The twenty-three-year-old was a visitor from Texas, in the town on a skiing vacation. Police believe it was murder.'

I turned the radio off. Scott came back to me. I thought about the first time we worked together.

'Flick?' said Scott. 'That's a funny name.' We were in a police car in downtown Denver.

'Well, my real name's Felicity,' I said. 'My dad liked it. There was an English movie star called Felicity. At school everyone thought it was very funny, so I became Flick.'

'Flick Laine,' he said.

'Yeah, good, don't you think?' I said.

'Yeah, Scott and Flick,' he laughed. 'Denver's crime fighters!'

'Hey, don't you mean Flick and Scott?' I laughed.

Scott and Flick, Flick and Scott.

Now I looked at the road. I tried to think about the drive. The road was at 7,000 feet already. But it was a beautiful day in the Rockies. Really beautiful. The sky was clear blue and you could see for miles.

But I couldn't stop thinking about Scott. I thought about the day he died, in November, just two months ago. The day we went looking for Eddie Lang, one of Denver's worst criminals. He killed people for money. But we were on to him. We knew where he was.

We were in an old, dark house. We knew that Eddie Lang and his men were there.

'Don't worry, Scott, I'm behind you,' I said quietly.

I could see Scott in front of me. It was dark, but I could just see him. Suddenly I heard a loud noise. A gun. Then Scott was down on the dirty floor. His blood was everywhere.

I ran outside quickly and called the police station. A few minutes later more police officers arrived. But Scott was dead. Scott was dead and Eddie Lang and his men were gone. They were gone, but I thought about Scott every day.

I went on driving. An hour later I drove into the parking lot of Pine Crest police station.

Something told me that Bill Gershon, Chief of Pine Crest Police, wasn't happy to see me. 'So,' he said, as I walked into his office, 'Leo sent me a *woman* ...'

'Yeah, aren't you lucky?' I said, smiling. Gershon didn't smile. I sat down. There were still men in the police who thought that women police officers and murder didn't go together. It looked like Gershon was one of those men.

'We don't often have murders in Pine Crest,' he said.

I looked at Gershon. He was a round person: round body, round face, round glasses. About fifty, fifty-five maybe, with almost no hair. Then I looked around at his office. Yeah, I thought, parking tickets, not murder.

'Listen,' I said. 'Why don't we make this easy? Just tell me what I need to know.'

The Chief of Police said nothing for a moment or two, and then went on. 'Janine Anderson was her name. A student from Austin, Texas. She wanted to write for a newspaper – to be a journalist. This is about her.' He pushed some papers towards me.

I looked at the papers. There wasn't much. Her name, her parents' names. A student of journalism at the University of Texas, Austin. Cause of death: drowning.

'Her parents were in Europe on vacation.' Gershon shook his head sadly and said: 'They're coming back today. Coffee?'

It wasn't much, but it was a start.

'Who found her?' I asked, drinking the hot black coffee.

'Her friend, Teresa Douglas,' said Gershon. 'They were staying at the Mountain Hotel.'

The Mountain Hotel was in Pine Crest. A lot of skiers stayed there.

'They skied all day,' Gershon went on. 'Janine went to the swimming pool at about nine o'clock. The pool is on the top floor of the hotel. She had to go upstairs and go outside. At eleven o'clock the Douglas girl went up to look for Janine. She found her in the swimming pool.'

'Dead?' I asked.

'Yes,' said Gershon. 'Teresa Douglas tried mouth-to-mouth. Then we had a 9-1-1 call at about eleven-fifteen. We were there five minutes later. Janine was dead.'

'Did Janine have other friends here?' I asked.

'Yes. Apart from the Douglas girl, there's a guy – Jeff Mason,' said the Chief of Police. 'They're students in Austin.'

'Anything on the body?' I asked. I wanted to know if there was a fight before Janine died.

'On the back of her neck,' said Gershon. 'It looks like maybe somebody just put her head under the water and drowned her.'

'Well, we don't know that yet,' I said.

'This is terrible!' said Gershon. 'Governor Johnson is visiting Pine Crest soon. A murder is the last thing we need!'

Clark Johnson was the Governor of Colorado and everyone said he was the next President of the United States. He lived near Pine Crest.

I looked at Gershon. He wasn't thinking about the dead girl. He was thinking about the bad news, I thought.

I finished my coffee and stood up. 'OK, I'm going,' I said. 'Here's my cell phone number.' I wrote down my number and gave it to Gershon. 'I'm staying at the Pine Lodge Hotel.'

Gershon came to the door with me. He still didn't smile.

'Listen,' I said. 'Maybe you don't like it, but we have to work together. If this is murder, we have to find this killer before he, or she, kills again.' I looked at Gershon and walked away.

Great, I thought, just what I need – a Chief of Police who doesn't want to work with me. I went back to my car, took out my winter coat and put it on. It was cold here, much colder than Denver. We were at 9,000 feet. But it was a beautiful, clear day and there was a smell of wood smoke in the air. I walked down the road to the Mountain Hotel.

I looked at the town. It was a pretty place. Behind the small houses were the big houses of the famous people who lived in Pine Crest. Lots of movie stars and famous sports people had homes there. Sometimes you saw them on the ski runs, in the stores or in the more expensive restaurants in the town. I looked up to the snow-covered mountains. I could see ski runs everywhere, but there were only a few people moving down the mountain. It was a beautiful day for skiing, cold and clear. But no-one wanted to ski. They thought that there was a killer free in the town.

Chapter 3 *The Mountain Hotel*

Then I saw the Mountain Hotel. I walked into the hotel and looked over to the bar. There was a fire; it was warm and comfortable. It looked nice, I thought.

Janine Anderson's friends, Teresa Douglas and Jeff Mason, were in Room 203. They were about twenty-two, twenty-three years old. They looked young, lost.

'It's terrible,' said Teresa. Her face was wet. She cried softly. Jeff sat down next to her on the bed and put his hand on her shoulder.

I looked around at the room. It was Jeff's room. From the window you could see a very high mountain, the one they called Snowpeak. There were clothes everywhere, ski boots under the window.

'We can't believe she's dead, ma'am. It's terrible,' said Jeff. When he spoke I could hear that he came from Texas. He was a tall, blond young man, good-looking.

'I understand,' I said. 'I'll try to be quick, but I have to ask some questions.'

'Sure,' said Jeff.

'It was eleven o'clock,' Teresa said, 'when I went to look for Janine.'

Teresa looked up at me. She had dark hair and very white skin.

'You slept in the same room, you and Janine?' I asked.

'Yes,' she answered, 'me and Janine in one room, Room 309, and Jeff in this room.'

I looked at the girl. I gave her time to tell her story.

'Janine went to the swimming pool at about nine o'clock. I fell asleep at about ten-thirty. I was very tired; we skied the whole day. But I woke up just before eleven o'clock and saw that Janine wasn't there. In her bed, I mean. So I got dressed and went up to the top floor. It was really cold outside. I saw her in the swimming pool. Just on top of the water.' The girl put her head in her hands. 'I can't stop thinking about it,' she said. She was quiet for a moment.

'I jumped into the pool,' she went on. 'I tried to pull her out of the water, but she was too heavy. I turned her over and put my mouth to hers, but it was no good. I knew it was no good.' Teresa put her head in her hands again and cried.

'And there was no-one else around?' I asked after a few minutes.

'I couldn't see anyone,' she said. 'I shouted out and a hotel worker heard me. He called the police.'

'And was Janine a good swimmer?' I asked.

'Oh yes, ma'am,' said Jeff. 'She was a great swimmer. I'm sure that Janine didn't drown by herself.'

'And how long have you been here?' I asked.

'Almost ten days,' said Jeff. 'We have to leave tomorrow. Classes start next week.'

'And do you want to write for a newspaper, like Janine?' I asked.

'Yes, I do. I study journalism,' said Jeff. His face went white. 'Janine wanted so much to be a writer,' he said. 'It was the thing she wanted most in the world. And she was really good.'

'We know each other from the ski club,' said Teresa. 'We all loved skiing.'

'Is this your first time here in Pine Crest?' I asked.

'Mm, yes it is for *us*,' said Jeff, 'but Janine knew it; she came here every year. To ski, I mean. She was the one … She said it was a lovely place. And it's true. We were having a good time here.'

'Did Janine know anyone here in Pine Crest?' I asked. 'I mean, did she see anyone while she was here – a friend – anyone?'

Teresa shook her head. 'I don't know,' she said. 'I don't think so. Just us, I think.'

'But she sometimes went off on her own – alone?' I asked. 'Like the night she died?'

'Yes. Janine always went to the pool alone in the evenings,' said Teresa. 'But she didn't talk about anyone. I don't think she knew anyone here. I think she just thought, or wrote in her notebook, and went swimming.'

'Notebook?' I asked.

'Yes, Janine wrote in her notebook every day,' said Teresa. 'She wrote about her day, about her thoughts, her feelings, I think. About things that happened to her, things she saw. Like Jeff said, she wanted to be a writer. She liked to write.'

'And where's her notebook now?' I asked.

'Well ...' said Teresa, 'in our room, I think. She always kept it next to her bed. She liked to write when she woke up in the morning. You know, her dreams and things. Do you think it could be ... Shall I get it?'

'We can all go,' I said.

We all went upstairs to Room 309. It was the same as Jeff's room, but with two beds. Teresa looked for the notebook.

'I can't find it,' she said. 'It isn't here!'

'It must be somewhere,' said Jeff. 'Shall we help you look?'

'Well, OK,' said Teresa, 'but it isn't here. Really, it isn't. She always kept it next to her bed!'

We looked everywhere in the room. But Teresa was right. Janine's notebook was gone. Perhaps she took it with her to the swimming pool last night? I left the dead girl's friends with some questions in my head. Where was Janine Anderson's notebook? Did Janine Anderson's killer take it? And if so, why?

Chapter 4 *A talk with Jeff*

I went upstairs to the swimming pool where Janine died. From there you could see everything: the town and the mountains. Two of Gershon's men were there.

'Were you here last night?' I asked the men.

'I was, Detective Laine,' said one of them, a tall, big guy. 'The name's Williams. Sergeant Bob Williams.'

'And did you find anything?' I asked.

'Just a pen,' said Williams.

'A pen?' I said.

'Yes,' he said. 'I found a pen just here by the side of the pool. They're looking at it – to see if it was the girl's.'

It looked like Janine Anderson really was writing in her notebook last night, I thought. The pen was there, but where was the notebook?

'OK. And one more thing,' I said. 'Can you get to the swimming pool without going through the hotel reception?'

'Yes,' said Williams. 'You can go through the parking lot, and the place they keep the skis, then into the elevator.'

'And the elevator brings you here?' I asked.

'That's right,' he said.

'No security cameras?' I asked.

'No,' Williams said. 'I talked to the hotel manager and he told me they never had any problems.'

Until now, I thought, as I left the Mountain Hotel.

I went outside into the street. On a wall there was an advertisement. 'Governor to run for White House,' it said.

There was a picture of Clark Johnson, the Governor of Colorado. The elections for President were later in the year.

I looked back up to the top floor of the Mountain Hotel. I couldn't see the pool or Williams from here. But maybe from higher up? I looked across the street and saw a restaurant called the Columbine. You could sit outside at the top and I could see people at the little tables. I went in and walked up the stairs.

I showed the young waiter my police badge. I looked over to the Mountain Hotel. I could see Sergeant Williams next to the pool. What if…? The killer could see Janine Anderson from here! He could sit here in the restaurant and wait, then just walk into the hotel.

'Last night,' I said to the waiter, 'did you see anything … anyone strange?'

'Strange?' The young man thought for a moment. 'Mmm,' he said, 'well, there was one man … he's come here every night for the past ten days. A slim guy, about thirty-five, always alone. Sits here for hours sometimes.'

'And last night?' I asked.

'Last night,' the waiter answered, 'I thought it was strange because the man asked for coffee but he left before the coffee came.'

'He left without paying?' I asked.

'No, no,' said the waiter, 'he paid. He left some money on the table and just ran out.'

'What time did he leave?' I asked.

'Oh, I can't remember, I'm sorry,' said the waiter. 'We were busy last night, but we close at ten.'

'What time do the waiters leave?' I asked.

'Oh, usually about ten-thirty,' he said.

So maybe the man just walked across the street, through the parking lot and into the hotel to kill Janine Anderson? And no-one could see him from the Columbine because it was closed. Was the man at the Columbine Janine Anderson's killer?

I left the Columbine and walked back to the police station. I told Gershon about the man at the Columbine. 'Get Sergeant Williams on to it,' I said. 'We need to find that man.'

I got in my car and drove to my hotel. The Pine Lodge Hotel was just half a mile away from the Mountain Hotel. I usually stayed at the Pine Lodge when I came to Pine Crest for a skiing weekend. It was a friendly place with nice, comfortable rooms.

From the window of my room I looked out over the mountains. Then I opened my small suitcase, lay on my bed and thought about what I knew.

It was easy for the killer, I thought. Easy to watch Janine from the terrace of the Columbine. Easy to get to the swimming pool. But why?

I turned to the phone on the little table by the side of the bed. I called Leo and told him what I knew so far.

Leo listened. Then he asked, 'How's Bill Gershon?'

'He's surprised I'm a woman,' I said. 'You didn't tell him …'

Leo laughed. I laughed too. We talked a little and then Leo said: 'Flick, I have something to tell you.'

'Yes?' I said.

'We found out something today about Eddie Lang and Scott's murder,' said Leo.

I sat up quickly and shouted: 'Eddie Lang! You mean you know we can get him?'

'Wait,' said Leo. 'Not exactly, but I think we're very near.'

'I'm coming back,' I said. 'I need to be there.'

'No,' said Leo. 'You stay right where you are. We'll get Eddie Lang. You get Janine Anderson's killer.'

I felt weak. I said goodbye to Leo, put the phone down and lay down again. It was only three o'clock in the afternoon, but I felt tired and closed my eyes. Before I knew it, I was asleep. I dreamed about Scott, like I often did. I dreamed about his blood on the floor.

Then a noise woke me. It was the phone.

'Hello,' I said. My voice was heavy with sleep.

'Detective Laine?'

'Yes, who is it?' I asked.

'It's Jeff Mason – Janine's friend,' said the young man. 'I have to talk to you.'

'OK Jeff, sure,' I said. 'Come over.'

I got up and took a shower. I tried to wake up, tried to forget Scott's blood on the floor. The redness of it. I let the water fall over my body. It was warm and it felt good. Scott was dead, but the water felt good. Ten minutes later Jeff arrived. I went down to Reception to see him. We sat by the fire.

'What is it?' I asked.

The young man looked at me. 'Well, maybe it's nothing, but ...' he started. I could see that he really wanted to talk.

'Well,' I said, 'it's best to tell me if you think it's important.'

'It's about the notebook,' he said.

'The notebook?' I asked. 'Do you have it?'

'No,' he said. 'No, it's just that ... Well, you know that Janine was studying to be a journalist?'

'Yes, like you,' I said.

'Well, I was thinking ...' Jeff said.

'What is it?' I asked.

'The thing is,' he said, 'every year at our university we have a competition.'

'I don't understand,' I said.

'It's a competition for students of journalism,' he told me, 'in February. It's for the best story. You know, something new ... something that no-one knows about.'

'And?' I asked.

'So the winner – the one who writes the best story – gets a big prize,' he said, 'and Janine really wanted to win.'

'And she was good ...' I said.

'The best.' Jeff smiled. 'And she was working on something really big, I'm sure.'

'How do you know?' I asked.

'Well, I just know she was,' he said. 'She was always writing in her notebook. I could see she was. It was something big. And I'm sure it was something about Pine Crest!'

'Why do you think that? About Pine Crest, I mean?' I asked.

'Well, you know she came here every year?'

'Yes,' I said.

'I watched her,' said Jeff. 'Well, you know, we were friends. And she went to the library at least two afternoons in the last ten days, after skiing. For books. She was trying to put the story together. I'm sure of it!'

I thought about what he said. 'But she didn't show it to you?' I asked. 'Or talk to you about it?'

Jeff smiled. 'No!' he said. 'I'm in the competition too. I don't know if it means anything … that the notebook is gone.'

'Well,' I smiled at him, 'it's something.'

I looked out of the window. The mountains were soft and quiet.

'Why didn't you say something before?' I asked him.

'I didn't think … I mean I didn't think it could have anything to do with it,' said the young man. 'But maybe it does. And now the notebook's gone.'

It was quiet for a moment. Then Jeff spoke. 'You know, Detective Laine,' he said, looking at me, 'it's really terrible to lose someone close to you. I can't tell you how I feel … I feel terrible.'

'Yes,' I said. 'I know.'

I looked at Jeff. He looked so young and so sad. I don't know why, but I wanted to tell him about Scott. Perhaps it was because my dream was so close to me. Perhaps it was because Jeff had kind, blue eyes. Perhaps it was because Jeff's friend was dead too. I told him the story. The story about Scott.

'We never caught him,' I said. 'Eddie Lang, I mean. I never caught him. I knew it was him. I knew he killed Scott. But ...'

'But you didn't have anything ... you couldn't show that it was him,' said Jeff. 'I understand. Yes, it's difficult.'

'Yeah,' I said, standing up. 'Most days it's difficult, and some days are more difficult than others.'

'So ...?' Jeff asked.

'So how do I live?' I asked the question for him. 'Well, some days I think why wasn't I there in front? Why didn't I die? Then some days I think why didn't I stop Lang, stop him from shooting Scott?'

Jeff looked at me.

'But most days,' I said, 'I think we're going to get Eddie Lang! One day, Eddie Lang will be in prison for a very long time!'

Chapter 5   *Looking for reasons*

That night at about nine-thirty Janine Anderson's parents flew into Denver International Airport. They were returning early from their holiday in Italy. A police car drove them to Pine Crest Hospital. They had to see their daughter's body, to see that it really was Janine.

The Andersons were staying at the Pine Lodge too, and late in the evening, at about eleven o'clock, Bill Gershon brought them to the hotel. 'I'm so sorry,' I said to them. 'I'll try to make this quick.'

Gene and Loretta Anderson were both forty to forty-five, well-dressed, rich Texans. Janine's mother soon went to her room and I talked to the father. Gene Anderson was a Texas oil man, a man who was now very rich, but who started life on a farm, a ranch, near Houston.

'I just can't believe it,' he said again and again. 'She was so young, so intelligent. Who did this, Detective Laine? Who killed my baby?'

'I don't know, Mr. Anderson,' I said, 'but I am going to find out.'

'I hope so, Detective Laine. I really hope so.'

'But I need your help, Mr. Anderson,' I said.

'Anything I can do,' he said.

'Well, there is one thing,' I said. 'She was studying to become a journalist, right?'

'That's right,' he said, 'and she was an "A" student.' He smiled for the first time. 'She was a really good writer,' he said. 'All her teachers said she could be a really good journalist one day.'

Gene Anderson tried to stop himself from crying. I waited for a few minutes.

'Mr. Anderson, Janine's friend Jeff told me that she was writing something for a university competition,' I said.

'Yes,' said the dead girl's father, 'and she really wanted to win. She wanted to be a journalist more than anything in the world. And she knew that it was a good start. She told me something about it at Christmas.'

'Did she tell you what she was writing about?' I asked.

'No, not really, ma'am,' said Gene Anderson, 'but I think it was something big.'

I looked at Gene Anderson.

He went on: '"Daddy," she told me, "this story's so big it's going to get me the journalism prize and maybe somebody will go to prison for a very long time."'

'But she didn't tell you who the "somebody" was?' I asked him.

'No,' he said, 'she didn't. She was working on it, you know, getting it right. Hey, you're not saying …?'

'I'm not saying anything, Mr. Anderson,' I replied. 'Nothing at all.'

*   *   *

The next morning I got up early and went out. It was very cold in the early morning. The snow was hard and it was difficult to stay on your feet.

I thought again about what Gene Anderson told me. 'Somebody will go to prison for a very long time,' his daughter said to him. Who was it? What was Janine writing about?

I looked for Pine Crest Town Library, the library where Janine Anderson went to study for her story. Then I saw a building with a big sign outside. It said: 'Books can change your life.'

I went into the library. The young woman at the desk had big hair and a big smile. 'Good morning, can I help you?' she said.

'Yes,' I said, and showed her my police badge. 'Detective Flick Laine, Denver Police Department. It's about the death of Janine Anderson.'

She stopped smiling. 'Oh yes, poor girl … it's terrible.'

'Did she ever come here?' I asked.

'Yes, she did,' said the young woman. 'She mostly wanted to look at pages from old newspapers.'

'She could take books and newspapers away?' I asked.

'She had a letter from her university,' said the young woman, 'so she could take newspapers and books out. She was a student, you know.'

'Yes,' I said. 'Do you have a list of the newspapers and books she took?'

'Oh yes,' said the librarian. 'Would you like to see it?'

'Yes, please,' I said.

The young woman turned to the computer in front of her. 'Here,' she said. 'Have a look.'

First, there was the dead girl's name and home address in Texas. Then there was a list of books; all of them were about Colorado and land development. Then there was a list of about ten newspapers that Janine took from the library in the last two years. I asked to see them all. In every newspaper there was a story about ski resorts and hotels. One of them talked about a famous movie star.

The movie star, Susan Hunter, who lives in Pine Crest, said: 'People have always come to Colorado, to get rich fast. In the past it was gold and silver. Today, most of the gold and silver has gone. The new gold is land that can be used for ski resorts and hotels. Land developers make millions of dollars from this land. Today in Colorado, there's a fight between big business and nature lovers who want to stop this. I am fighting for Colorado!'

I closed the newspaper. Big business, I thought. Big money. Every year in Colorado there were more houses, more stores, and more ski resorts. More and more people trying to make money. I knew that people who lived here in the Rocky Mountains often got angry. 'This is nature,' they said. 'We don't need more buildings. We don't need more ski resorts.' But it was like standing on the beach and trying to make the sea go back.

Chapter 6   *A movie star*

I called Gershon on my cell phone.

'Susan Hunter,' I said. 'She seems to be very active in the fight against land development.'

'Yeah, she *was*,' he said. 'But she hasn't done anything for a while.'

'Where does she live?' I asked.

'Big house up on Hillside,' he said. Hillside was the part of Pine Crest where all the famous people lived.

'Good,' I said. 'I'll go to see her. Oh, and did you hear from the hospital?'

'Yes,' he said.

'And?' I asked. Working with Gershon was slow.

'Well, they are sure now that it was murder,' he said, 'and it was a man.'

'What time did she die?' I asked.

'Between ten-thirty and eleven,' he said.

Janine Anderson died minutes before Teresa Douglas went to the pool and found her body. And probably minutes *after* the waiters at the Columbine left.

I put my phone away and felt my gun in my inside pocket.

At three o'clock that afternoon I parked my Chevy next to Susan Hunter's Jaguar, outside her beautiful big house. Movie stars, I thought. They don't like development, but they live in big houses!

I got out of my car and looked at the mountains. I saw that there were cameras everywhere around the house. A very tall man came to the door. I could see that he had a gun under his jacket.

I showed him my City of Denver police badge.

'Good afternoon, Detective Laine,' he said, smiling.

He took me into the star's living room. A few moments later, she walked in.

Susan Hunter was a beautiful woman in her thirties, with black hair and clear blue eyes. She was dressed in grey trousers and a red blouse with a high neck. We sat together in the very big living room, drinking tea. Around the room, there were photos of the star with other famous movie stars. There were also photos of her husband and three children.

'Yes, in the past it was gold and silver, Detective Laine,' she said, taking a drink of her tea. 'Now it's ski resorts. There's always some reason why we need land.'

I waited for more.

'But,' she said, 'it can't go on like this. The land is not ours. It's for our children and our grandchildren to enjoy. This is such a beautiful place.'

'Yes, it's lovely,' I agreed. We looked out of the window. The sun was starting to go down over the Rocky Mountains and the sky was pink and orange.

'But ski resorts mean big money,' she went on, 'and it's difficult to stop people buying and developing the land.' Her voice became very quiet. 'Look at Redridge,' she said.

'Oh yes,' I said. Redridge was a small town thirty miles away. It was an old silver town.

'Well,' she said, 'three years ago Redridge was a small, quiet town. Now it's a very big resort with hotels, expensive stores and restaurants, and ski runs everywhere. It has thousands of visitors every year.'

'So?' I asked. 'Isn't that good for the town?'

Susan Hunter laughed. 'Have you seen it?' she asked.

'Tell me more,' I said.

'The Government Land Office,' she said, 'bought the Redridge land fifty years ago. Then, in 1997, they – the GLO – wanted to sell the land. They knew they could sell it as a vacation resort and get a lot of money.'

I knew that this happened a lot. The government was always trying to find ways to make money. Susan Hunter went on: 'So they asked vacation resort companies to tell them about their plans for the town. There were five big companies that wanted to develop Redridge. The company that won was Alpine Resorts. Their boss is a guy called Ricky Klein.'

'Ricky Klein?' I asked.

'He's always in the newspapers,' she said. 'He's very rich and he has hundreds of businesses. Alpine Resorts was already famous for Alpine Resorts Oregon, which destroyed beautiful natural forests. Three of the other four companies all had good plans for Redridge. They wanted to save its natural beauty,' she went on.

'So why did the GLO choose the worst plan?' I asked.

'Ha! That's the big question, Detective Laine,' said Susan Hunter. 'I guess that Ricky Klein gave someone in the GLO a lot of money.'

'Money? A bribe?' I asked.

Susan Hunter nodded. 'A bribe,' she said. 'Millions of dollars, I guess.'

'And why wasn't it in the newspapers?' I asked. 'I mean, you knew about it … who else?'

'The GLO kept everything quiet until the last minute,' she

said. 'Then it was too late. My group was called Save Colorado. We knew about the bribe from someone who worked for the GLO. But we don't know who took the bribe.'

I looked at her. 'Did you know Janine Anderson?' I asked.

'Yes, I did a little,' she said quietly. 'She came here to talk to me last year. I told her what I knew.'

That's it, I thought. Janine Anderson found out the name of the person in the Government Land Office who took the money.

It was quiet for a few moments.

'And what about Pine Crest?' I asked.

'Well,' Susan Hunter said, 'the next Alpine Resorts development will be in Pine Crest, later this year. What happened to Redridge will happen here. They'll kill its natural beauty.' She smiled sadly. 'And no-one can save it.'

I stood up to go. At the door, I turned round. 'There's one thing I don't understand,' I said.

'You mean why don't I do something about this? Why didn't I tell the police before now?' she asked.

She pulled down the neck of her red blouse. On her neck, very near her throat, there was a big scar. From a knife.

'Detective Laine, I have three children, a wonderful husband and my work,' she said. 'I don't want to die.'

'What happened?' I asked.

'It was a year ago. Oh, I can't say who it was,' she said. 'It happened at night and I didn't see his face. But I'm sure it was because of all this. These are dangerous days. We must be very careful.'

Yeah, dangerous days, I thought. I felt my gun under my jacket and left the movie star's house.

Chapter 7 *A visit to Redridge*

I drove away from Susan Hunter's house and back to my hotel. I thought about my talk with the movie star. Ricky Klein of Alpine Resorts gave someone in the Government Land Office a bribe to take the worst plan for Redridge. And Janine Anderson knew all about it. But who was it, and how did Janine find out?

I went back to my room and called Gershon.

'Bill, I want a full list of people in the Government Land Office since 1996. Can you ask one of your men to get it for me?'

'I guess so,' said Gershon.

Same old Gershon. What was wrong with the guy?

The next morning I woke up early. I picked up my gun. I remembered Susan Hunter's question about Redridge: 'Have you seen it?'

It was time to visit Redridge. I wanted to see it for myself.

I got in the Chevy and drove the thirty miles to the town.

'Welcome to Redridge, home of Alpine Resorts Colorado' said the sign as I drove in. The town was busy with people on vacation. Skiers, mostly. On Main Street there were some stores and restaurants. Then, at the end of the street, I found the beginning of Alpine Resorts Colorado. At the gate was a man in a blue uniform.

'Good morning, how can I help you?' he asked. He smiled and showed very white teeth.

'Well,' I said, 'I'm just visiting, you know, and I'd like to take a look.'

'Of course,' he smiled. 'I'll ask someone to show you around.'

I waited. He talked to someone on the phone. A few minutes later a young blonde woman walked up to me. She smiled a lot too.

'Good morning,' she said, shaking my hand. 'My name is Tina Nielson from Alpine Resorts. Let me show you around our beautiful resort.'

We started walking. Alpine Resorts Colorado was almost like a small city. When you went through the big gate there were a lot of different buildings. There were three swimming pools, four hotels, vacation homes, restaurants and ski rental. It was very, very big.

'We have the complete vacation here,' smiled Tina. 'You can do everything. You don't have to leave Alpine Resorts.'

I looked around. Many of the buildings were so big that you couldn't see the mountains.

'Yes,' she went on. 'It's a vacation for the whole family. And the skiing is very good. We have all the ski runs in Redridge right here.'

'You mean,' I said, 'if I want to ski I have to stay here?'

'Well,' she said, 'of course you can ski just for the day. But the ski runs are ours. I mean Alpine Resorts'.'

'And how much is a ski pass?' I asked.

'It's three hundred dollars a day,' she said.

Three hundred dollars! That was double the cost of a ski pass in Pine Crest. Alpine Resorts was very expensive; someone was making a lot of money!

'But why don't you try it?' she said.

'Well, I'm a little busy …' I started.

'Come on,' she said. 'We'll be happy to give you a half-price ski pass for the morning. That will be just seventy-five dollars.'

'Well, OK,' I said. I could ski for an hour or two, I thought. I needed some time to think.

I went to the ski rental, and got some skis, boots and poles. I went up the mountain on a ski lift and spent an hour or two skiing the lower runs. It was a beautiful day to be on the mountains. But from the top I could see how big Alpine Resorts really was.

At about eleven-thirty, I went into a café halfway up the mountain. There were a lot of other skiers there. I drank my coffee, took my ski run map out of my pocket and looked at it. Up above the café there were some difficult, 'black' runs with interesting names like Mad Dog and Killer Run. I wanted to try them. And I wanted to get away from the people. I needed to think.

I took the Mountain Tops ski lift up another 1,000 feet. Here, at 10,500 feet, the world was white and quiet. It was very cold. There were almost no people, just a few figures far away. Most skiers stayed down below. I felt alone. I put my hand in the pocket on the inside of my coat and felt my gun.

I wanted to go up even higher, to 12,000 feet, almost to the top of the mountain. I started to walk slowly to the Summit ski lift. Suddenly, I heard somebody behind me.

'Detective Laine,' said a man's voice.

I turned around. The man was wearing a black ski mask. I couldn't see his face. Just his brown eyes.

I moved away from the man quickly. But the man came closer to me and said in my ear: 'Turn around, Detective. We're going to get on the ski lift together.' I felt something hard in my back. It felt like a gun. There were no people, anywhere. Just the man with the gun and me.

'And don't do anything stupid,' he said, 'or I'll kill you.'

Chapter 8 *Dangerous days*

'You can't do this,' I said to the man.

'Be quiet and get on the ski lift,' the man said. He pushed me.

The ski lift had a seat for two people. The man pushed me into the seat and then he got in next to me. I looked around, but there was nobody up here. The ski lift went up. Up to the top of the mountain.

I looked at the man, at his brown eyes. He was slim. Was he the man at the Columbine?

'Give me your gun,' he said.

'My gun?' I said.

'Come on,' he said. 'I know you're carrying a gun.'

I looked down. We were thirty feet over the snow.

'And don't do anything stupid,' he said.

I put my hand inside my coat and felt my gun. I took it out and gave it to him.

'And now,' said the man, putting my gun in his pocket, 'you're going to fall ... you're going to fall from the ski lift.'

'You're crazy!' I said. 'They'll catch you.'

'I'll just say that you fell,' he said. 'Anyway, I don't know you, and you don't know me, do you?'

I thought fast. 'I know you work for Ricky Klein,' I said, taking a chance. I needed time and I wanted him to talk.

The man looked at me. 'You're smart,' he said.

'And Janine Anderson?' I asked. 'Did you kill her?'

'We had to,' he said. 'She knew too much. She asked too many questions. And she was very stupid. She wanted to tell everyone about it.'

'How did you know that she was alone in the swimming pool?' I asked.

'I watched her,' he said, 'watched her for days.'

'From the Columbine restaurant,' I said.

'Yes, she often went to the pool alone in the evenings. It was easy. I just went into the hotel through the parking lot.'

Yes, I thought. It couldn't be easier.

'And then you took her notebook?' I asked.

'Do you think I'm crazy? Of course I took her notebook. I burned it.'

I didn't want him to stop.

'And she knew the name of the man in the Government Land Office?' I asked quickly. 'The man who took a bribe from Ricky Klein to let him build Alpine Resorts Colorado?'

'Yes, Detective,' he said, 'the Big Boss, Big CJ.'

'Big CJ? Who's that?' I asked.

'Enough questions,' said the man. 'I just do the killing, Detective.'

I looked down. We were very high. The snow and the trees were a long way down. I could see two skiers on the mountain but they were very far away. I couldn't shout. I couldn't do anything.

'You're next, Detective Laine,' he said. 'Time to die.'

I looked down again. It was a long way down and he was trying to push me. I had to do something and I had to do it now.

The gunman moved to lift up the bar on the ski lift. Quickly, I moved forward and hit him in his face with my right hand. At the same time, I hit his hand with the gun in it with my left hand. The gun flew out of his hand and fell. It made no noise as it fell into the snow far below.

'You ...' he started, 'you ...' But it was too late. I hit him on the back of his head, pushed him and he fell. Down, down, down.

I looked down and watched him. His skis were heavy and he fell fast. He fell into the trees far down below. I pulled down the bar. The ski lift went on moving. Up, up. It was quiet again. The only thing I could hear was the sound of my heart.

Chapter 9 *A lot to lose*

'Whisky, please,' I said to Bill Gershon.

I sat down. It was nine o'clock that evening. We were in his office. I needed a drink. Gershon took the whisky from his cupboard. I smiled at him. 'Just like Leo,' I said. 'Do all Chiefs of Police have whisky in their cupboards?'

Gershon smiled and put the whisky down on the little table in front of me.

I took a drink of the whisky. It was good. I looked at Gershon. I was alive.

'Tony Rizzo,' I said to Gershon, 'what did you find out about him?'

The only thing I knew about the gunman was his name. The police found his body in the snow. Tony Rizzo was the name on the driver's license in his pocket.

'Tony Rizzo came from New Mexico,' said Gershon. 'He was a hit man for anybody who paid him.'

A hit man. A killer. And Ricky Klein had enough money to pay him, I thought.

Gershon went on: 'He spent four years in prison near Santa Fe, New Mexico, from 1993 to 1997 for killing a security guard.'

'Only four years?' I asked.

'He got out,' Gershon said. 'His friends helped him. He jumped out of a window and onto a furniture truck.' I looked at Gershon. He was almost enjoying himself, I thought. Well, it was different from parking tickets.

'Anyway,' I said, 'I got everything from him.'

'The whole story?' asked Gershon.

'Well, almost everything,' I said. 'I got Rizzo to talk on the ski lift. He killed Janine Anderson. And Ricky Klein was behind it.'

'Wow!' said Gershon. 'You're good!'

I smiled. 'That's the nicest thing you've said to me, Bill,' I said. Gershon looked at me and smiled. Maybe we were becoming friends at last.

'But there's someone else,' I went on. 'Someone Rizzo called the "Big Boss, Big CJ". Janine Anderson knew a lot. Everything, I think. About Klein, how he gave a lot of money to this Big CJ. This man who was in the Government Land Office.'

'Government Land Office!' said Bill Gershon suddenly. He put his hand in his pocket and took out about five pieces of paper. 'I forgot! Here are the names.'

I took the papers from Gershon and put them on the table in front of me. I read through them. I was looking for a famous name.

A few minutes later I looked up at Gershon. 'Bill, there's one name on here that ...'

'Yes, I know,' said Gershon. His eyes were big and round. 'Governor Clark Johnson ... a member of the GLO!'

'But it can't be!' I said.

Clark Johnson! CJ! The Governor of Colorado. And the man who everyone said was the next President of the United States.

I drank my whisky. Now I could see everything. 'Janine Anderson had enough to send Klein to prison for twenty years,' I said to Bill, 'and she had enough to finish Governor

Johnson. She wanted to write all about it. Of course she had to die.'

'But how did Janine know about Clark Johnson?'

'Maybe she guessed at first,' I said. 'She knew that it must be someone important in the GLO. Someone who needed a lot of money.'

'Wow!' said Gershon. 'If this is true, it's big!'

'Yes,' I said, 'it's big. Johnson was in the Government Land Office when Klein built Alpine Resorts Colorado in Redridge. Johnson needed money. He wanted to become Governor.'

'So Klein said, "You let me build Alpine Resorts …"' said Gershon.

'"And I'll give you money!" A lot of money. Millions of dollars, probably,' I said. 'We can look at his bank account easily enough.'

'And then Johnson wanted to become President!' said Gershon.

'Yes,' I said. 'I think Janine really did have a big story. The biggest.'

The 'next President of the United States' took money from Ricky Klein to let Klein build a new Alpine Resorts. What was bigger than that?

'But now we've got enough to send Klein to prison for a very long time,' I said. 'And I think we can get Clark Johnson too.'

'Wow!' said Bill.

'Yes,' I said. 'Wow!'

Chapter 10   *The Big Boss*

'That's the story,' I said to Jeff Mason.

Jeff now knew everything about Alpine Resorts and Ricky Klein. And about Governor Clark Johnson.

'So that's why poor Janine died!' he said. 'Because of Clark Johnson!'

'Yes, and now we need to get Johnson,' I said.

'What about Klein?' asked Jeff.

'We can't find him,' I said. 'He knows about Rizzo and he's gone – the police are still looking for him. We're going to get Johnson,' I went on, 'and I need your help.'

*   *   *

An hour later, Jeff called Johnson's office. I listened to the conversation on another phone. 'I want to speak to Governor Johnson,' said Jeff.

'I'm sorry, but the Governor is busy now,' said a young woman. 'Can I help?'

'Yes,' said Jeff. 'You can tell the Governor that I want to talk about my friend Janine Anderson and the money Governor Johnson took from Mr. Ricky Klein.' Jeff gave the woman his hotel name and his telephone number.

Now we just had to wait. We had to wait for Johnson's new hit man. Tony Rizzo was dead, but I was sure that Clark Johnson had another hit man. Another killer. We waited in Jeff's room. It was dark. Jeff was on the bed. Two of Gershon's men waited near the window. They had their guns.

I was behind the door with my gun. We waited one hour, two hours. It was late at night and the hotel was quiet.

Then I heard a noise outside the door. Somebody was trying to get in. The door opened and I could see a man. I moved fast from behind the door. Then I hit him over the back of his head with my gun. He fell to the floor like a tree. He didn't move.

I turned on the light. Gershon's men came out with their guns and stood around him. One of them took the hit man's gun from his hand. Jeff got up from the bed and came over.

I looked at the man on the floor. He was wearing black clothes and he had a black ski mask over his head. I took it off and looked at the man's face.

I turned cold. I couldn't speak. Jeff looked at me. 'Do you know him?' he asked.

'Yes,' I said quietly. 'It's Eddie Lang. The man who killed Scott.'

'Tell me about Governor Clark Johnson,' I said to Eddie Lang. 'He's behind this, right?'

Eddie Lang looked up and saw all the police around him. 'Yes,' he said.

*   *   *

The next day, I was in Gershon's office.

'We've found Klein,' he said. 'He's told us everything.' Bill Gershon smiled at me. 'Thanks, Flick,' he said. 'Thanks for everything. I'm sorry ...'

'Forget it,' I said, smiling.

I said goodbye to Gershon and the others – to Jeff and Teresa, and to Janine Anderson's parents.

'Thank you,' said Gene Anderson. 'Thank you so much.'

Then I got in my red Chevy and drove out of Pine Crest and onto the highway. I looked back at the beautiful Rocky Mountains. The mountains were white and the sky was blue. Life was almost good. Janine Anderson's killer was dead. Ricky Klein was going to prison for twenty years and Alpine Resorts was finished. Better than that, Clark Johnson, Governor of Colorado, was finished too. He could never be President of the United States now.

I thought about Scott. I could feel him smiling at me. 'Good work, Flick,' I could hear him say.

And, perhaps best of all, I thought, Eddie Lang was going to prison for a very long time! Yes, life was good. I was in my red Chevy and life was good.